Raking Leaves

ISBN 978-0-9832589-1-9

Raking Leaves

poems

Joseph Grantham

Holler
Presents

Also by Joseph Grantham

Tom Sawyer

for
Bud & Rae
and
Scott & Julia
and
the people of Northampton County

"You're a poet. Welcome to hell."

– JAMES WRIGHT

Poems

l

introduction

by the time you leave here
you are going to think
everything is a poem

raking leaves

get me in the thing
the thing in the room
over there
and then get me
get me out there
out there on the lawn
with the rake
raking leaves

squad goals

i feel like if i can finally grow a beard i'll look like fat jim morrison and it'll be good

i like hotels

i like hotels

desire

i don't want anything
actually
actually i do

on the way to the trail

you got an exception
i got an acceptance
no a rejection
from a literary magazine
they made the biggest mistake
of their lives
i'm gonna kill 'em all

nature poem #1

smells good
out here

math

i got a bad attitude about math
i do too

morning poem #1

you should take the antipsychotic
seroquel

what would it do

it wouldn't do anything to you
it'd just put you down

john deere

my landlord's dad is in a wheelchair and he mows my
lawn

belk

your mama handed me garments
she said, *ain't this soft*
and i said, *yes, this is soft*
she held up a dress to your chest
this looks like ashleigh
but i didn't think it looked like you
i wanted to be at home on the bed
watching the baseball game and learning big words
i don't know enough big words
even now i can't think of any
and i've had all day

doomsday

today i drove by the doomsday prepper's bunker
today a man with no legs in a motorized wheelchair
drove by me

chestnut street

she catches me looking at myself in the mirror so i blow
out my cheeks like a puffer fish

nature poem #2

yep
yep
yep

good deed

i was gonna write
all these letters
to all the coworkers i liked
before i quit
and left my job
in new york city
but then
i just never did

(laughing)

death of america

nothing like
smoking a cigarette
looking at a foreclosed house
watching a dog take a shit
drinking
diet mountain dew
diet citrus drop xtreme
diet dr. k
diet mountain lightning
sometimes la croix
or coffee
but never water

three bumper stickers on
one car in reno, nv

swastika
confederate flag
'i love my dachshund'

warning

i write poems
about massacres
minutes after they happen

sitting on leaves

we shot the bb gun
at the cantaloupe
and at the soda cans
and then we watched a movie
and ate pizza
and then we went to sleep
and while we slept
a man killed
fifty plus
with some rifles
in las vegas

apology

i got a little bit
political
in my poems
today
sorry

kroger reflection

should i be spending this much on soda

buzzard

i hit a buzzard with ashleigh's car
but it was okay
it got back up and flew away

courtland, virginia

i ran over a turtle in the middle of the road
i tried to straddle it with your car
but i missed
and it felt like running over a rock
but it was a turtle
and we talked about it for a little while
before we got to the renaissance fair
you asked me if i wanted you to warn me next time
you saw a turtle in the road
you told me that any time we're near a stream or creek
i should watch out for turtles in the road
and i was upset because i tried to straddle the turtle
and because when i first saw it
i thought it was a piece of trash
i didn't want to run over the turtle
it was an accident
and when we got to the renaissance fair
i didn't like it
and i didn't like the knights and the swords and the funnel cake
and there should be a nat turner museum in courtland, virginia
because that's where the rebellion happened
but there's not a nat turner museum
there's just a renaissance fair

julia's poem

in california
you cannot pick the nature
in west virginia
they let you pick the nature
and take it home with you

thurmond, wv

good
old
coal

occupations

i can't tell you what my mom does
i know about as much
as a six-year-old would know
about what my mom does
i know what my dad does
because it's not complicated

just wanted to make it right

now he knows
how to make
the
coffee good

he knows
how to make
coffee good
now

he knows
now
how to make
coffee good

he now knows
how to make
the
coffee good

now he knows
how to make
the
coffee good

he knows how to make the coffee good

how'd you sleep

okay well you sleep tight

see you in the morning
or in the afternoon

there you go

he slept fine

she couldn't sleep last night
she thought she had spiders
crawling all over her

i couldn't sleep last night
i thought i had
lung cancer

ahoskie

ever since i read in the local paper that an old man was
beaten up in his bed in the middle of the night i've been
worried that i will be beaten up in my bed in the middle
of the night

scott's family tree

i come from a long line of wayne
middle names

what's your grandma's
middle name

wayne

what's your dad's
middle name

wayne

well what's your
middle name

wayne

gas station

don't write about
no girlfriend
feeling fat
any kind of loneliness

instead
buy candy bars
and packages of candy
and

rake leaves
rake leaves
rake leaves

jelly's song

go pee pee poo poo
go pee pee poo poo
go pee pee poo poo

goddamnit

go pee pee poo poo
go pee pee poo poo
go pee pee poo poo

good girl

tudor's biscuit world

it's a small world

scott's discovery #2

not all corporate things are bad

look at
mountain dew
and
cigarettes

farewell

we should
go to
chili's sometime

ll

bank robbery #8

i was a professional baseball player
known for my bunting
she pronounced boise like
'boy-see'
i pronounced boise like
'boy-zee'
someone could have written
a song about us
it would have been a hit
and it would have made
no sense
one year she got really into poetry
and she made me take her to readings
and there was one reading
where they charged us at the door
something like twelve bucks
can you believe that
twelve bucks
to listen to some people read some poems
and after the reading
i pulled her aside
and said
'i've got a poem for you'
i said it menacingly
but what happened was
i gave her a kiss
a dry peck
where am i going with all of this
we were in love
and we never went to another poetry reading
and we were on our way to the bank

bank robbery #2

when i wake up
i check my email
and if there are no new emails
i rob a bank

i've gone four days
in a row
without a new email
so that's four banks robbed

if i don't get a new email soon
i'm either going
to get caught
or get rich

bank robbery #7

all you need is
a car
and a gun
or something
that looks like a gun
sometimes it's better
if it just looks
like a gun

bank robbery #5

my name is rob
and i work at the bank
i was there
you know
when it all went down

bank robbery #3

carl had a gun
and marla was carl
except the 'c' was an 'm'
and she tacked on the 'a'
because she liked decorating
the christmas tree
oh and she also had a car
and so they got along
and away
for a while
but they were found
and carl used the gun

III

pharmacy poem #1

writing a poem
writing a poem in a pharmacy
writing a poem in a pharmacy in north carolina
writing a poem in a pharmacy in north carolina in
america

pharmacy poem #16

people die a lot

pharmacy poem #7

it's hard to write a poem
at the pharmacy
the pharmacist is behind me
and he puts medicines
on the counter
and he can see
over my shoulders

poems

poems are coins

aunt sandy

i almost tripped over the cat
her mother and father survived the holocaust

poem for ricky

ricky likes my girlfriend
he has a produce stand
and he makes his own ice cream
and every easter he carries a cross for a mile
and he likes my girlfriend
ricky told her he liked her lipstick
and he told me he hoped i didn't mind

woodland

you tell me about your dream
i'll tell you about mine
i can't remember mine
i'll drive you to work
then i'll come home
and look for work
i can't find anything
i'll do pushups
while you do policies
then i'll pick you up from work
we'll go get dinner
i'll have what she's having
she'll have something else
we'll ask the waitress
if she's ever heard of 'ahoskie'
and go see a movie
stop at big jim's
on the way home
not for pig feet
let's split a gatorade
and ask the attendant
if she's ever heard of 'woodland'
get home late
wine and tea
write postcards
and stretch
and i guess
i'll see you in the morning

rich square

the people of rich square walk in the middle of the road
and one day i'm going to kill somebody

pharmacy poem #19

the ladies i work with said i could put them in my book
if i made them skinny

august 6th

your sister started seeing that state trooper again
and now we don't see her anymore
but we saw her yesterday
because it was your birthday

your mama wanted to be the first
female state trooper
in north carolina
but her daddy wouldn't let her
so she became a parole officer
and then she worked at the ABC store
and then at the pharmacy
and then i stole her job

writing workshop

i'm going to take you down
to the abandoned casket factory
that burned down a few days ago
and that's it

neighbors

the ones over there don't buy groceries

hot dog

i'm not really a hot dog guy

her husband

he's got a skin cancer on his back and it's pulling all the skin off

pharmacy poem #20

brenda asked me if i knew how to get a snake out of the
ceiling of her trailer

binker

i had a cousin named binker but he died

nerf gun

not everyone in my neighborhood gets a poem
especially not the kid with the nerf gun

burp

the parking lot goes on forever
until it doesn't

i'm happy to be here
until i'm not

spruce street

ashleigh's mom lives across the street from the parents of
the girl who put her baby boy in the trash

pharmacy poem #8

i got my coat today
and ashleigh nailed
blankets to the walls
to keep us warm

tammy wynette

can we borrow
your mama's plunger
we don't have one
we only have
that other thing
i'll walk over there
and get it
and then we can
fix this toilet
i shouldn't have
dumped the litter
in the bowl
i shouldn't have
taken all the keys
off my keyboard
there are so many things
i shouldn't have done
don't make a list

possum

i need a new pair of socks
no i want to kiss you
should i get that tv from my mama
i guess
when you moved
he fell off the bed

the mcdaniel farm

i asked you what your favorite part
of the poem was
and you said
'when he goes down to the mcdaniel farm'
but there was no mcdaniel farm in the poem
and there never will be

pharmacy poem #5

my back hurts
stop buying medicine from me
stop needing medicine from me
i'm just a kid
i'll never have a career
i don't know what i want
to be when i grow up
across the street
in the parking lot
cooks and waiters smoke
stray cats start families
and the grocery store next door
doesn't work anymore

poem for luis

luis is from jalisco, mexico
he waits tables at los amigos
in ahoskie, north carolina
he always shakes my hand
and brings me tortilla chips
he has a nice smile
we can hardly speak to each other
i will show him this poem

poem for doctor stanley

a 92-year-old doctor who smokes cigarettes in his office
prescribed me antibiotics for my throat
he was a volunteer firefighter
he built his own coffin
i walked to the funeral
they brought his coffin to the cemetery on a firetruck
after it was over they set off the fire alarm
and all of their walkie talkies crackled and buzzed
wooooooooOOOOOOOOooooooooooooooooooooooooooo
we don't have a doctor in our town anymore

rhonda

rhonda drove us to the airport
i'm not supposed to talk about rhonda
i paid her to take us to the airport
it's my job to not talk about rhonda
it's rhonda's job to not be talked about by me
rhonda used to write
she said the words stopped coming to her

what i see

there's the woman with the beard
she's going back inside the family dollar

norfolk

for a long time
i didn't know that
fruits are comprised
of carps
there is a pericarp
an endocarp
and an exocarp
also a mesocarp
there is even a man
sitting across from me
with a haircut
drinking a coca-cola

pharmacy poem #9

i have a lot of days off
thank you susan

pharmacy poem #2

i made the coffee
too strong at work
and everyone hated me
and then i spilled the coffee
on my white coat
and everyone hated my coat
but it was christmastime
in my head
so i walked down the street
to the dollar store
and i bought some of those crackers
the fluorescent orange squares
with the peanut butter
around here
they call them
nabs

meatballs

she's downstairs making dinner
because we got mad at each other
she doesn't want me
to throw the honey into the cupboard
she wants things to be organized
i made her a peanut butter and honey and banana and
apple jelly sandwich
i was going to use that as an excuse
i was going to argue
but i went upstairs
sat in the room i used to sleep in
before i started sleeping
in her room
tried to read a book
imagined running into the next room and opening the
door and jumping
off the balcony
thought about a broken leg
sitting on the wet grass screaming
for her to stop making meatballs
for her to come outside and look at me
for her to fix my broken leg
or take me to the hospital
but i don't jump off the balcony
i go downstairs
and i eat the meatballs

pharmacy poem #6

a man bared his teeth at me
he was smiling
he was a state trooper
or he worked at the jail
or he bought a newspaper

feel bad

i poured hot water on an ant

mac

'the ballad of the green berets'
came on the radio
and he laughed

i never saw them do much
i was in the marine corps
we did recon
so we were out in the jungle
listening
and then we'd call in an air strike
blow up a village
come back the next day
and do it again

love poem

give me your hand
hey wait a minute
we were eating breakfast
i don't like when they butter
the toast for you
i'd rather do it myself
my father is the same way
he gets upset
when he loses something
he drives around busy parking lots
praying to saint find-a-spot
and i know that
any life can feel too long
i'm thinking about the carpool again
i have to apologize
i do this a lot
but i was rude to you
you used the last coffee filter
i had to use a paper towel

ladybug

i found a dead ladybug at work
but i did not bury it

pharmacy poem #11

dell had multiple sclerosis
i talked to him two days ago
today he shot himself in the head
his dad found him
a helicopter took him somewhere
he died plugged into something
probably better that way
tomorrow he was cremated
tomorrow tomorrow
we can talk about something else
it'll be someone else

pharmacy poem #10

i had a bad sleep
i woke up cold
she had some teeth pulled
she talked funny
she applied for assistant manager
at the new grocery store

motorcycle

i will buy you a motorcycle
but if i buy you a motorcycle
you have to ride the motorcycle
and you have to take me
with you sometimes
i like quality time
even if i can't hear you
and i'm on the back of a motorcycle
and i'm holding on to you
and don't ask me
if i'm scared
i'll tell you if i'm scared
okay i'm a little bit scared
sorry for asking you
what you're afraid of
that was a big question
to ask someone
while sitting on a rug
that is older
than both of us combined

pharmacy poem #15

i am eating peanuts in the pharmacy
i am eating ginger snaps in the pharmacy
i am eating crushed ice in the pharmacy
i am eating yogurt in the pharmacy
i am making decisions
kansas is playing on the radio
bachman turner overdrive is playing on the radio
michael mcdonald is playing on the radio
america is playing on the radio
i am sitting on a stool
there's nothing else for me to do

joyce carol oates

i went upstairs
so i could
write a poem
for you
it's cold
up here
we live in the middle
of everywhere
tomorrow i might
go to new jersey
which is in the middle
of nowhere
some old lady said
thousands of people
don't know how to read
and some young woman
is going to kill her

pharmacy poem #3

i made that chocolate cake
and i was
employee of the month
over at perdue
you don't want a job
in a chicken factory
i get so tired
driving to work at three a.m.
i forget to take my medicine
and you call me crazy
but i got three days off
and a $50 gift card to walmart

poem for the squirrel

she wants me
to write a poem
for the squirrel

the squirrel
had trouble
crossing the street

i drove her
to work today
and yesterday
and tomorrow
i don't have one
i need to get one

i saw a dog
hear a ringtone
and its ears
perked up

i heard these guys
hammering on a house
sounded like a game
of ping pong

when i had a job
my dad gave me
a paper menu
to a barbecue restaurant

and i didn't know
what to do with it

at home i walk
around in my underwear
it's hot in this house

she's bad
at drinking water

she wants me
to write a poem
for the squirrel

the squirrel had trouble
crossing the street

i used to write poems
about bank robberies
i used to commit
bank robberies

i drove her to work today
i don't have one
i need to get one

i saw a dog
hear a ringtone
and its ears pricked up

i heard these guys
hammering on a house
and it sounded like a game
of ping pong

she wants me
to write a poem
for the squirrel

the squirrel had trouble
crossing the street

i drove her
to work today
i don't have one
i need to get one

i saw a dog
hear a ringtone
and its ears perked up

i heard these guys
hammering on a house
sounded like a game
of ping pong

at home i get to
walk around in my
underwear
it's hot in the house

she's bad at drinking water
i have the opposite problem
and i'm always in the bathroom

pharmacy poem #18

i change my mind about susan
she started taking a lot of days off

pharmacy poem #14

i don't eat big enough breakfasts
i drive by trailer parks on my way to work
his brother called but he didn't want to talk to me
so i passed the phone around until it landed on someone
good
juan is dead
his brother found him
i liked juan
he thought the fbi was after him
he changed his name every couple of years
he looked like robin williams and he laughed like
juan is dead

the man who brings me eggs

i used to write
'pick up son from school'
on the back of my hand
so i'd see it on the steering wheel

pharmacy poem #17

he came right up to the counter
rattled off all the places he'd been
raleigh
bali
norfolk
iraq
he served in the military
he paid his mama's bill
and bought a bar of dove soap
and when he left
the pharmacy technician who likes my hair
told me he'd really been to all those places
and he fought in iraq
and something exploded by his head

diner poem

i'll never be afraid of death
when my time comes i'll just eat
a sandwich over the kitchen sink
this poem is not accessible
i put a formica tabletop in the poem
and it isn't enough
so i build a diner
and i put the diner in the poem
i'm eating eggs in a booth
at the back of the poem
i like it here
because i own the place
and the service is good
because i am the service
the food is only okay
because i am the cook
i don't leave a tip
i don't even pay the bill
and when i'm done with my eggs
i press a napkin to my mouth
and the grease from my lips
is a rorschach blot
i toss it onto the plate
wring my hands and look at the clock
at the front of the poem
everything in here is
crimson and turquoise and chrome
because i couldn't think of anything else
but you see it and me
i leave through the back door of the poem
because that's the way i came in

pharmacy poem #4

it doesn't matter who you are
you will marry
a woman named kelsey
there's no need for you
to be consoled
kelsey is great
remember you met
in middle school
everyone you've ever met
you met in middle school
please enjoy your life

Joseph Grantham is the author of *Tom Sawyer*.
He lives in America.

Made in the USA
Lexington, KY
25 November 2019